Aegis of Waves

Aegis of Waves

Elder Gideon

atmosphere press

I dedicate this collection to all my kids.
Thank you for letting me in.

Contents

In the space we make

#MARCHFOROURLIVES

Awaking with a start,
the President was shaken.
By a dream that no one,
his cabinet nor any
his soothsayers, could interpret,
save some youths imprisoned,
famed for dream interpretation.
He summoned them. To tell him
what it meant—

"

I was in the Astrodome
filled with thousands gathered.
intermittent power caused
arena lights to flicker.
When the lights went out,
you couldn't see a thing.
Instead of football on the field,
Every one was looking up
armed and aiming at the ceiling.
Where I stood made hard to see
their target in the smoke.
When I looked below, I saw so
many piled up empty cages.
Then I knew that every person
there was shooting for a prize.
When the lights would blink back on,
their guns would fire all at once.
Rounds of shots erupted like
a dozen awful bombs that
stung my ears and seared my eyes.
No one turned to see one fall
down maimed or dead from ricochet.
No one shouted out
for help that never came.
I saw others no one noticed
Doing something strange.
Standing there with walking sticks.

They waited 'til the lights went out
And all the shooting stopped.
It fell quiet.
Enough to hear another speak.
In that darkness spoke the name
another one nearby.
Gently held his ear.
Natural that it drew their eye
away to look out to their side.
Though they didn't know this
other speaking, something opened.
Do I know you? he would ask,
Of course you do! Remember when—?
So they'd talk like neighbors as
shooting all around resumed.
So engrossed in stories long
forgotten, the one who heard his name
had set his gun down at his side,
unaware it turned into
a walking stick. On they talked.
Face to face like two old farmers
resting hands on tops of handles.
As lights went on, they turned away
To face another near them. Waited
for the quiet of the dark to
speak another's name.
On this went, as one by one,
responding to their names,
others paused to hear their name
and reminisce until their rifle
turned into another stick.
When lights returned, I finally glimpsed
the birds that flew above us.
rounds exploded everywhere
as people fell from ricochet.
In and out the cloud of gun smoke
up against the metal dome
flashed a convocation.
Fledgling eagles crying out
against nowhere to go.
My heart sank where I stood,

so powerless to stop.
Feathers snowed as shattered wings
could no more lift the air.
I witnessed many eagles fall
To mauling crowds that fought
and brawled like savage dogs.
Lights blacked out in riot kills
That chill me still to tell.

What say you, youths,
the meaning of my dream?"

Uno

Wheezing in its drought the sun
Fluoresces orange outside
Our classroom windows drift
Sparks of dust encircling the world

Most my Muslim students' seats are empty
This holyday their faces laugh from house
To house this Eid Al-Adha *Allah*
Commanded Ibrahim to offer
His son Ishmael Ibrahim said Yes

The remnant of my English-learners wait
In their seats upon my humanity
Their unspoken plea behind twelve pair
Of brown eyes dare imploring me from
Syria Rwanda   Burma Venezuela
Mexico Nepal   Afghanistan Iraq

Theirs are the plaintive faces of any
High school kids their last class
On the Friday before Labor Day as
Gad caught my glint Anisha tested it
What we gonna do? I answered Yes
—Play Uno
Jenga or joking Wash my car?

In two minutes three groups of four
Turned their desks to face each other
Out came the basket of Uno decks &
Tunes & jokes laughing from hand to hand
As our air-conditioned room eased
Us all into the simple good
Indwelling dust encircling the world

YOUTH DETENTION FACILITY   *For DS*

panting glass facade
under ticking clocks
click hands leaking sand

HAT AND PHONE PLEASE. WHO
ARE YOU HERE TO SEE?
—D.S.   RELATION?

  —His teacher. I'm on
his visiting list.
PLEASE WAIT TO BE CALLED.

I ease my breathing
inside this fortress
to keep my heart unguarded

THIS WAY.
EEEEEEE

I strip all metal
EEEEEEE

I move to stop
EEEEEEE

through lock upon lock
EEEEEEE

my feet are adrift
EEEEEEEE

through cement hells
EEEEEEEE

I'm shit out the final canal
into an open clearing of glass rooms

Your brows rise surprised to see me approach
as my heart sags YOU HAVE FIFTEEN MINUTES

to see you marooned younger brown and thin
dwarfed behind glassed within

if walls have ears, these have eyes all knowing
we've not much time

we sit at either side of a mirror
without silver. Framed enamel wall tanks

slightly constrict with no natural light
or sound. Your voice comes delayed through a grill

in the glass. In solidarity, I speak

       —'s good to see you. Good to see you too.
       —We all miss you at school. Both our eyes brim.
       I miss everyone too. Thank them for me,
       the peer mentors, everyone who listened.
       —I will   *I care about you* More than
       I can say   I see your ember remains
       As your mentor, I ask you to hear yourself
       walk it back to the moment it happened.

You paused and began to speak of the weed
in your bag the VP's first search request
then campus police's second request
the third (each time escalating the fault line
driving brown & black bodies facedown)

I resisted arrest. He put his hands
on me. I black out when men put their hands
on me. Reminds me all my mom's boyfriends.

Listening with my eyes to honesty
in yours dissolved the glass wall between you
and me, you and yourself facing this world

—This is real men's work, I speak —to know
Their only enemy's inside their own heart.

    —I'm proud of your courage
       YOUR TIME IS UP
     to know your part.

We both stand   I put my hands to your hands
to the glass that's dissolving in our gaze

Far away you'll soon be moved to live with
mom and who-knows-who I'll never see you

I reach through to embrace this man within
a son of a son. Too many are gone.

I leave. I drive. I grieve
The hell we call normal.

PREFRONTAL CORTEX

Harm draws on our young
Shame us all intolerably
We're weary always correcting
They game too high they fall too far

They often climb up over us
Their bodies bend the canopy
From which they look out over
Distances we never dare

To the trace looming smoke overhead

Their cries scatter birds
They leap and swim about the limbs
Restless every burning stirs them
We know we have to move

Burnings force us all to move

Harm outgrows our young
What we have they do not want
Who seem to sense before there's smoke
They have to go

We have to let them go

There to live where they're to go
Running into skulls of smoke
Forests burning in their limbs
They will climb blinded

Harm will show our young
To outwit flame survive as prey
Too bold too cautious too quick too slow
Or falsely judge the edge of death

Will claim the ones we someday find
Underfoot our forward haste

NAHUA RITES OF PASSAGE NORTH

♫ Que triste se encuentra el hombre cuando anda ausente
Cuando anda ausente muy lejos de su patria...

How sad one finds the man when going away
when going away so far from his homeland...

(Aguilar, "Paso del Norte")

As seeds on either side of streams,
On winds through fences none outrun,
We glide like our maternal tongue.

You're someone
Among Nahuas
Only when you've left us
And made yourself
unauthorized   *No autorizado.*

[United] States En los *Estados*
are our male northerners *Son nuestros Norteños,*
       Our sons made men.
on the other side Al oltro lado.
You also, daughter *Tú también, mi'ja—*
Make yourself a woman *Que te hagas mujer.*

There's only *Hacer*
to struggle. To make *La lucha. Buscar*
a living. Beyond *La vida. Mas allá*
the border   *La frontera.*

La Despedida — The Farewell—Separation

Your spirit guides agreed.
      —You will leave.

So let us supplicate
La Guadalupe.

Pray She promises
That all goes well with you.

On your behalf, we offer
Her flowers & votives—

For your safe journey, pray
She receives our feasting
Dance and singing.

Here. Take her rosary—
Your abuela's.   *grandma's*
Pray our dead might
Guard & guide your way

Someday to *el norte.*   *the north*
Family awaits the other side,
Your embrace of you remains

La siguiente canción   *The following song*
está dedicada a ——   *is dedicated to* ——
de parte de sus padres,   *from her parents,*
que esperan que la escuche   *who hope that she hears*
y sea de su total agrado...   *and loves it...*

El Viaje —The Journey—Transition

How destiny
can make one weep

♪ *Ay que destino,*
 para ponerse a llorar

The faintest falsetto in the wind
From hundreds of miles behind her
Was all her tears could hear.

Between sunrises on her right,
And sunsets on her left,
Nothing else was sure but *Coyote*   *smuggler*
Driving her across the desert.

Whatever was in the trunk of their car
That brought her to this freight depot
Was enough for Coyote to trade it
With a *narco* speeding out of sight.   *trafficker*

Coyote led her to the farthest building
Back along the train tracks where
There was no sleeping day or night
in the roaring of LA BESTIA.   *"The Beast" train*

Narcos occupied these buildings,
Demanded absolute silence
From everyone packed between
Infested walls. Unless the door opened,

There was no sight outside this dark,
But for the one time people panicked.
Narcos hissed and abused them,
Tore one out the door by his hair.

No one heard the narco or the man
Over LA BESTIA thundering by
Until the narco kicked the door in,
Holding up a dripping head—

La Recepción—The Reception—Incorporation

♫ *Uuuyjaja, Adios mi Mexico,*   *Goodbye my Mexico,*
Adios mi Mexico

Beneath the turning vault of heat & dark,
She crossed the bleaching barrier.
Blistered, she staggered from the car door
To McDonald's. Coyote's only word to her

Toward the bathroom hall was,
Sit there, *Siéntate allá*, pointing
in the bathroom stall—
Don't come out until I whistle. Her heart

Pounded between the walls when black
Migra boots prowled in & paced.   *police*
Steel toes sniffed the desert on her shoes.
They paused, unable to hear her heart

Hammering. While the boots turned &
Stepped out, the sun slipped down
Beneath the city's skin into the underworld.
Coyote whistled fluorescence.

She hatched from within the walls.
He took her hand to front as her boyfriend
To walk forty sprawling blocks of dusk
Beneath the smatter of stars cities allow.

Swollen heels stepped over flashbacks.
A cement treadmill turned past neon grease,
Storefront window irons grinning black,
Her skin worn thin as the soles of her eyes.

Coyote stopped here in front of this dismal
Motel wheezing mute with dimly-lit
Silhouettes in doorways. Up the second story,
Coyote smelled his prey. Five thousand paid.

She turns and follows up the steps toward
the standing silhouette whose scent of songs
from home long gone opened border doors.

IFTAR GHAZAL *for AA*

When I'm triggered by your temper, I remember
Your neighbors desperate to find where you'd been

buried alive in rubble. They lifted you like a bloody doll
With its head broken open. When I see your scar, I lean

Into you, the miracle you are living. The imam you will be
Are yet my student knocking afterschool outside my routine.

Your fasting shamed my fatigue and shifted my mind
To my heart. I helped correct your grammar of a scene

Of your diaspora from Iraq to America. Your older brother
Almost made it until Feds suspected him in between

Syria and Turkey. The FBI invaded your tenth birthday,
Took him from your arms through a torn door screen.

FBI vans swallowed him behind iron as you wailed away.
You were dashed again to the ground as a broken figurine.

From your own rubble, as for any refugee your age,
The test of jihad is inside, where Allah alone shall intervene.

To fight outside is to have already lost the fight inside.
You opened my heart to what Islam means.

I too regard you as family, as a son. In Ramadan,
you welcomed me, to break the fast at sunset, to convene

With the men of your mosque. Here I am a sojourner
in response to the Lord of the Universe, *Rab el Alameen*.

Alongside you I bow to the light of all prophets,
to the Most Gracious, the All-Merciful One. Amen in Amin.

Our life is a space

Palindromic

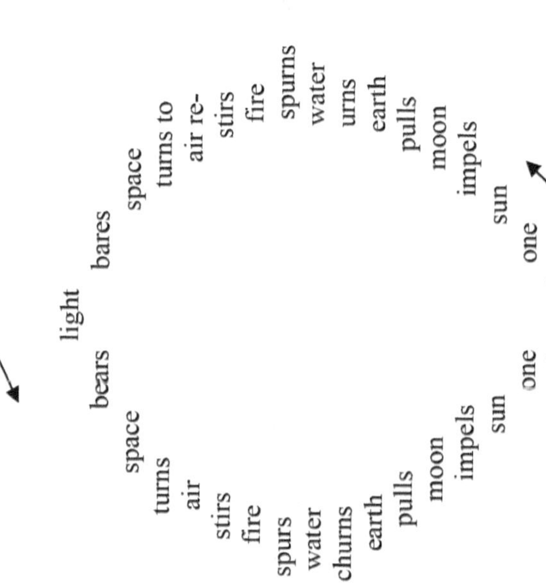

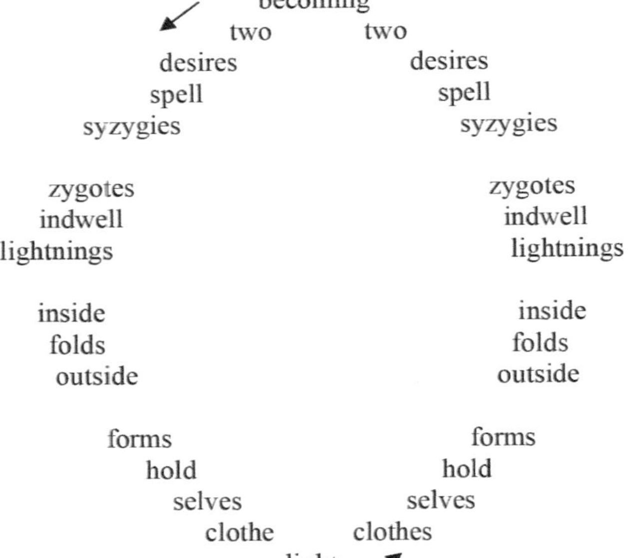

becoming
two   two
desires   desires
spell   spell
syzygies   syzygies

zygotes   zygotes
indwell   indwell
lightnings   lightnings

inside   inside
folds   folds
outside   outside

forms   forms
hold   hold
selves   selves
clothe   clothes
light

CONJUGAL

<table>
<tr><td>

I am
you are
he/she/it is
we are
you are
they are

I was being
you were being
he/she/it was being
we were being
you were being
they were being

I had been
you had been
he/she/it had been
we had been
you had been
they had been

I will be being
you will be being
he/she/it will be being
we will be being
you will be being
they will be being

I would be
you would be
he/she/it would be
we would be
you would be
they would be

</td><td>

I am
you are
he/she/it is
we are
you are
they are

I have
you have
he/she/it has
we have
you have
they have

I had
you had
he/she/it had
we had
you had
they had

I will
you will
he/she/it will
we will
you will
they will

I would
you would
he/she/it would
we would
you would
they would

</td></tr>
</table>

being	I was
being	you were
being	he/she/it was
being	we were
being	you were
being	they were
been	I have been being
been	you have been being
been	he/she/it has been being
been	we have been being
been	you have been being
been	they have been being
been being	I will be
been being	you will be
been being	he/she/it will be
been being	we will be
been being	you will be
been being	they will be
have been	I will have been being
have been	you will have been being
have been	he/she/it will have been being
have been	we will have been being
have been	you will have been being
have been	they will have been being
have been	I would be being
have been	you would be being
have been	he/she/it would be being
have been	we would be being
have been	you would be being
have been	they would be being

VALENCE

Amid these buildings blinking outside
Of all the windows why this one

Pressing me to its water-stained glass
Its bed sheet curtain clipped askance
Pulls me through its floral x ray print lit

By tv blue light inside sputters
Its pulse as compulsion
I pass beneath the valance to

Witness silhouettes twining in a bed

My headless face tapers in perspective
As gazing between two black mirrors

Frame me in her and him
Wherein their narrow lintel
Whose pulse in our compulsion

I slip within their valence

I | א *My Name is Adam*

& I'm ungendered. Wait—Zohar 3:296a
Don't flee this bathroom because of me
Fear silvers every mirror engenders dream. Stay—

let the faucet run Look closer at me
What sex are they your weary eyes?
What grief is your labor?

Before anything was face-to-face
I walked about back-to-back
unconscious of union in the garden

I desired nothing really, until a deep sleep
came over me and I dreamed *Elohim*

sawed me in two   a female and a male,

and presented me apart from a bone
from a bone from a flesh from a flesh
from a *helpmate* for and against me

I dreamed of a man from a woman
from the world outside from inside
this mirror here   from you and I

the story never said I woke

ungendered *offspring* dream   genes
they *grow within* the beginning   embryogenesis

unconscious of their single stalk
beneath stamen apart from carpel

like when Adam undivided
named every *kind* in the garden,   gene

where *spouses* halve   gametes
into *colored bodies*   chromosomes

whose waters *join*   zygote
in *threads* of light—   mitosis

heavenearth—
a *mulberry* cleaves   morula

the hollow *sprout* folds   blastula
into *viscera* concealing   gastrula

what's yet to be she or he
in iridescent *motions*   hormones

formed *in* every   en-
sort of fetal dust   gender

III | ג

                      Stay—
here with this bathroom mirror.
Let them come and go, in
 and out their flushing metal stalls.

The story never said I woke

but dream of two who blame
the other of themself,
          of Elohim for making, desire
who told you were naked

the fig leaves coats of skin

The story never said I woke

but dream behind your eyes
mirror mine   see as far
from one end of heaven to its end
as near within these bathroom walls
who told you were naked

MENARCHE

First she took breath from the opening.
Now opening takes her breath
Unknowing how the uncut moon bleeds

Red iron from novae flow ova.
As the force of life in full flower
Panics this child no more an androgyne,

Free of sin or gravity but over
Shadowed now by mortality. Looming
Is her well now deep as the moon her loom

Now longs for one pollen thread to weave and
Breathe into something new. For telling you,
Slap her face for the hardship of life

She'll face, or tell her father she is
Marriageable, or feel honor for her
Shamed discovery, or teach her of

Eve's penalty, or scar her and her
Betrothed in their parity, or enthrone
Her publicly in holy shade, or sing

And praise her fertility, or bathe her
Silvery in the pond, or seclude her
In synchrony with her sisters, and *go*

Within yourself say Yurok women *in*
This height of your power. Retreat from
Everyday things. Gather your energy.

Make yourself stronger in the purpose of
Your life. Earth has her own moontime. Go to
The moon. Talk to her. Ask her for balance.

(Thomas Buckley, 1988)

Female Initiation Rites

Widen my hips burgeon my breasts
Darken my groin—

I am the weal of descendants
Ancestors wheel about my nave

Cut their lines and circles
not on a tree stone or bone but me

I show by the iron in my blood
Running from eternal symbols etched in my flesh

That I am the earth speaking to you now

▽

In our daughters stirring She dreams us

We are Her ways She taught
She is our ways we keep

In every daughter's bloom She dawns
From soil for crops to grow

Our hearts need only feel with their fingers
To know how She is here

∇

Rouse her who left us take her limp hands
Lift from where she's come silence speaks

Join her to us sing songs to our brave traveler
Touch from where she's come time unties

Embrace her to us meet this woman who left a girl
Behold from where she's come changes everything

Feel her with us gaze into the eyes of our young envoy
Receive from where she's come goodness floods

One
Surrounds two

:

Birth
Earth
Growth
Death

:

In me the serpent meets the egg

From me come men

I am the awareness of ignorance its end

:

My birth womb conceives

:

My earth womb breathes

:

My growth womb weaves

:

My death womb receives

:

TO RUN

We are all watching   her family watches
Between you and us waits a whetted blade

Held at your foreskin

If you flinch blink make a sound even twitch
We will gasp out loud in shock and dismay
If you move *a-kwet*
              you ran a coward

Shamed will you be we as well all our line

A boy who runs
Makes his family depend
Forever unable to give
To have to eat their respect

We must not depend

Our not your blood runs

———

(Tepilit Ole Saitoti, 1986)

MALE INITIATION RITES

enemies anytime everything
nothing gives of itself nature tests
hunger and thirst is to be alive
if you fall back in fear we will die

your world is still her little hut
because you're blind you cannot see
what waits to wrest you from her arms
beyond her bed and soft embrace

every male worth seeding must resist
running back into the arms of his
mother's hut feminine mysteries
ceased the night you awoke in your dew

if you refuse to stand and fight
or know what pain it is to live
before your burning eyes you'll see
your kin be swallowed whole and end

where will we be without testing you?
women are born into women but
men are not born but are made into
men who must turn their face to the threat

we show a boy what life is like
to tear him out his mother's womb
to seize and strip him down by force
to face the task awaiting him

whip his legs lash his face tear his ears
sear his skin scar his back make him bleed
It is not we who test not at all
life is far harsher than warriors

MIS QUINCES

II

¡Damas y Caballeros! Y Ahora—
a proud daughter dawns in el Norte's promise
of opportunity into a princess—
presentamos nuestra quinceañera…
at the top of the stairs a tender vista—
all a migrant family could ever express
is lavished upon her, sparing no expense
beyond their means for all at this fiesta.
Her formal court of fourteen girls and boys wait
on either side below with every guest
breath taken by her twinkling in pink tulle lace,
her highlighted bride's face smiles brightly blessed
to step into love's applause for the innate
woman on her sweet fifteen, full of grace.

This day for this Latina, is her debut
celebration of song, dance, and tradition—
older than debutant rituals taken
from the courts of conquistadors—that all grew
through prayers of every Aztec parent, who knew
surrendering their daughter to a certain
future of her choosing could bring to ruin
all their deepest hopes clinging to her as dew.
See Mami set the sparkling tiara
upon her daughter's head, hold and kiss her face.
See Papi now replace his daughter's flat shoes
with heels to waltz one last time in his embrace.
Feel in their gestures how pride and heartache fuse
with an ancestral Nahuatl aurora

I

as they clasp their daughter full moon in the palms
of their hands, praying for their open flower.

Hear her father: *It is as if you*
were an herb, a plant
which has sprouted, grown,
blossomed. It is as if you'd
been asleep and suddenly awakened.

Hear her mother: *My dove, my little one,*
My child, my daughter—life is dangerous
And you must be careful.
Behold the path you are to follow:

On earth we live, we travel
along a mountain peak.
Over here is an abyss,
over there is an abyss.
If you go over here or
there, you will fall.
Only in the middle
can you go and live.

Place this word, my daughter—
My dove, my little one—deep within
the secret rooms of your heart.

Guard it well.

Aztec ceremonial prayers from the *Florentine Codex*
quoted by Julia Alvarez (2007)

FATHERS WITH THEIR SONS

Blacktop evening early spring.
Open weight room doors for air—
Striding down the covered hall.
Metal fountain's all clogged up
Hard white stains and sunflower shells.

Drink and look out east to where
Asphalt courts are breaking up.
Gangs have tagged the poles for good.
Without nets, the backboards rust.
Chain-link fencing you could hop—
Dilapidated neighborhood.

Nothing could have opened me
Fifty, sixty feet away to
Something astronomical,
Difficult, phenomenal,
Spectral, rare as UFOs,
Disbelieving, literal—
A father playing with his son.

Father's lithe and still in shape.
Son's a toddler at his waist.
Face to face they shift their feet with
Footwork moves he slowly starts.

Bodies stepping mirroring—
Drills he teaches—unison—
Left to right in harmony
Right to left in unity.
Run and jump up. Just like this.
Toss the ball—now back to me.
Perfect! Bounce it this way! Go!

Barely shooting over head
Father highs his tiny fives.
His son is beaming like the sun.
The game is not what it's about.

The heart with which it's done endures.

Oxytocin floods their court.
They play and laugh in spheres of fire
That darkness cannot overcome.

LOST RITES

                                        Existence
is a series of passages from one age to another
wrote Van Gennep, analyzing the ritualized life   (1909)
of human development in traditional lineages.
In each culture, ceremonies for every individual
were marked what he called *rites of passage.*
By these, people developed fully in their society

through every physical change, so that *society
will suffer no discomfort or injury.* Another
pattern reveals phases within every ritual passage—
separation, transition, incorporation. Life
held continuous, sacred meaning for individuals
in community, despite their social position or age.

Without initiation rituals, fewer come of age
to a viable place of incorporation in our society,
making more painful, uncertain, *an individual's
transition from one status to another.*
This in part explains modernity's malaise. Life
for young people seems arbitrary as their passage

of fulfilling desires lengthens. Forbidden passage
through straits of longing can often damage
fragile psyches. Without myths to guide life,
disfigured youth reflect a dehumanizing society.
Youth culture reacts against exile as *other*—
exposing the trauma of becoming an individual.

Angry youth who push back, individuals
who unconsciously seek their rite of passage,
are just as vulnerable to approval of another
force that eats its young. The marginal vantage,
that *novices are outside society and society
has no power over them,* often costs their life.

Having shattered every spiritual way of life,
colonialism continues to splinter individuals
into tinier figments of an imagined society.
Without conscious, communal rites of passage,
Western storm and stress will only ravage
what's left of a way forward, one way or another.

     [Separation]

No wonder youths of our societal mirror rage
against serving life terms—others beneath
elite individuals—without passage out.

     [Transition]

We are heirs of our imperial society,
Are the aging cannibals of history—
Indigenous individuals sentenced to text passage.

     [Incorporation]

Societies that desecrate their sacral image
send individuals adrift through another
Far harsher passage in eternal, liminal life.

Sutter Buttes Haibun

Chave's seen the Sutter Buttes his whole life, but never from inside. He and the boys took a chance on spring break. To hike with me up the smallest mountain range in the world. No one can enter the Sutter Buttes without an endorsed guide. Few indigenous Californians desire to enter. When invited, many refuse from nightmares.

We're deeper in as the road, like the boys' talk, gets rougher. Chave jokes like a prisoner. I struggle not to smile. They see my eyes laughing in the rear-view. We all laugh harder. Now I'm not their English teacher, but a man driving a van of young men. They're *hood*. Their humor is harsher. Our guide wonders *How is this day going to go?*

Through each unlocked ranch gate, we're moving back in time. The interior grass and oak woodlands part past us. But leering eyes in all of the rocks above follow us below. For millennia, native people honored this austere embrace to hunt, gather, and worship. The Nisenan called this *Esto Yamani*. The Wintun called this *Onolai*. This crown of mountains. A world navel. Fierce spirits here amplify to break. Far too sacred for staying. Might be why many resident ranchers have struggled here with misfortune or die untimely.

We're passing through. These Buttes know my intention. A moment of elevation for angry, young men. Few have ever been above sixty feet. Our guide reminds us here that there were initiation rites. Tests. Vision quests. So he asks my boys to not talk but listen while they hike. We walk. Through lush mariposa lilies and grasses whispering between our feet. Chave eases in with the rest. Quietly following up the North Butte. I live to share this centering silence. We are a single-file corps lightening in ascent. Hours later, dark rock eyes allow us passage to our vista point.

Upon a stone cliff we sit. Our feet dangle in sky. These young men are poised. In awe at how it all feels above. A young red hawk calls. My heart responds.

Farmlands, failing towns,
quiver in miles of haze—
no where to go.

Chave tightly squints—
"I can't see where I'm from,"
          as scales fall.

AEGIS OF WAVES

Not once
 Does one fall
 In the same
Rain twice

Not once
 Does one step
 In the same
Stream twice

Not once
 Can one run
 To the same
Sea twice

Not once
 Does one rise
 To the same
Sky twice

Others answer after us

PUTRESSENCE

All conceive in flight
All are heir to air

Few are parent butterflies
More are parent common flies

Few are eggs that hang up high
More are eggs that lay down low

Few are larvae born above
More are larvae born below

Few are fed by what still lives
More are fed by what has died

Few will molt and spread midair
Most will molt in search of sky

Few souls hatch from chrysalis
Most souls hatch from carcasses

If I had not nearly died,
Bored my way out of what is dead

An essence in putrescence—
This iridescent slick—chose

Me to break out breathing
Far beyond my body

THEY THINK THEY ARE WHITE

No one was white before   (James Baldwin, 1984)
Coming to America.

When I tell my students of color
What I understand about Black
Life is that

They look up from their phones
With wide brown eyes as brows rise
To hear me say,

I don't,

Admitting one doesn't understands

I have you to thank, Mr. Baldwin
For God's words through your spirit

Never ceased to preach
Long after you left the church
Unworthy of its prophets

Of our plight in America
Will end as it began

II

By opting for safety instead of life...
[they] have brought humanity to the edge
of oblivion: because they think they are white: (Baldwin, 1984)

Flashing from your mouth
a lightning *sword*   (Hebrews 4.12)
Sharper than any two-edged word
Strikes the colonial skull
Piercing until it divides soul
From spirit, joint from marrow
Lights the fuse trailing down
The spine of civilized crime
Detonates the sacrum
Shatters Adam
Whose shards are the heart
Of darkness   Edom
Stripped naked by the light bares
Its account for all it's done
In twoness before the One.

There is no other

But the heart that judges
A nation divided against itself
Cannot stand

♫ In-SOM-n-ia!   Am-NE-s-ia!
God SHED his GRACE on THEE! ♫

III

The really terrible thing, old buddy,
Is that you must accept them,
And I mean that very seriously.   (James Baldwin, 1962)

Forgiveness for privilege
Is outside of time
My tribe the nonviolent
For whom I lay my life

You must accept them and accept
Them with love, for these innocent
People have no other hope

Of deliverance—
From the land of Egypt
From our house of slavery—
Is only from within *I am*
The Lord your God   (Exodus 20.2)

They are in effect still trapped in a history
Which they do not understand
And until they understand it,
They cannot be free....

If hidden in the other
Is everyone one of us
With nowhere to go
But God together

We cannot be free
Until they are free.

STORM & STRESS

How with engorged stamen and carpels
Will the flush of growth steel them
To endure in neurotic lockstep

What span is theirs to reach or aspire
Beyond urban shade cast by phallic steel
Rising and goading them into systems

By the sweat of their bodies the sighs
Of their mouths the tears of their eyes   (Pistis Sophia I:25)
Adulthood drives into dragon jaws

Against what embroiled gravity
Of anonymity can progeny
Of that lonely dyad escape unscathed

By corporate crypts social scripts
Stratify ratify contradict why
Little fish feed ever bigger fish

How shall young roots hold if shamed
By bodies mating by birthing faces
By eyes exhaling vacant gazes

Individualism vies
Through young rowers in wooden boats
To clear the vise of icefields

Or be crushed to pieces sinking
Join the detritus of unfinished
Business digesting existence

It Is What It Is

i

ii

Young trees drip birdsongs
Curbsides gleam appeal

Dewy streets power fountains
Of federal champagne

GI bills spawned this sprawl
Sparkling tract homes freshly

Loaned generated the equity
To redline the quality of life

At first signs of racial equity
Whites fly up and away

Leaving what is left in their wake
Is for others displaced

To endure the harsher shade
Of dilapidated traps

Of ceilings all night long
That drip on tenant heads

Inside schooled margins
Young people posture

Their voices bluster against
De facto segregation

The despair of ever-
Breaking gravity

Condenses micro-aggressive
Drops that drip and fall

From water-stained ceilings
Drip drops on student heads

That roll off some
And press on others

Stalagmites case minds
Learn early on

It is
What it is

If we believe with kids
Can turn aside the drip

An inch
Is still a difference

DIGITAL NARCOSIS

Echo's seated on a warped boardwalk
Bench but it's not the sea she sees or
Peeling nickelodeons boarded up.
Only her phone. Before going home
To squalling tenements decades ago
After sweltering factory work she could
Escape for some hours. Here in a rowdy
Vaudeville or dance hall to release
Her body's desire for space and air
Or return his glance between mixed race
Couples swinging hard. No urban din
Could later quell the swollen urge
To hear her pant his name in the back seat
Over the car radio. Whitewashed
Blues rocked segregated roots
Into vises between suburban walls.
TV screens televised national vice.
My Lai abroad. Riots at home.
Assassinating our own.
The only cultural authority
Is commercialized leisure
In which teenagers, entertainment
Industries, parents, reformers,
And government officials all jockey
For position and control. We   (Lisa Jacobson, 2004)
Are the product now. Identities
Commodified into pixelated
Pools drown Narcissus. He's faced down
Out of Echo's reach some yards away
Alone on his boardwalk bench.
Neither look up from their phones
To see each other. Nor hear
The sea level rising.

THE HOUSE IS ON FIRE

Adults who deny
What stuffs their mattress are wrong
To dismiss *the house is on fire*   (Greta Thünberg, 2019)

Your angst is just
As we've bequeathed you a flat earth
Capsized upside down

Its crumbling edge
Where none can stand
To see species sliding overboard

Into outer space their eyes
Blinking back in the dark
What you do to these you do to Me   (Matt. 25.25)

Darkness is not dark to You
Night is as bright as day
Dark and light to You alike   (Psalm 139.12)

Spiraling cycles of *apocalypse*   ἀποκάλυψις
Simply mean revelation
The global agony of giving birth

Pangs rend curtains reveal
The real from unreal the outside
From the inside the unjust from the just

As any time before only now
The deadline won't relent
What's right buys time

Won't slow down until the end
Save for remnants who stayed human
Will remain to begin again

Not those who fear hell
Nor those who desire heaven
But all who love God

Everywhere want to stay
To serve is salvation here
Where hells grow heroes

EPILOGUE: TEXT BY AN ANGEL

This is not visible and invisible
This heaven of martyrs

Isn't to be misunderstood as only those
Who literally died in history for the faith

But also to include those whose entire life
Was about what's going on

When our lives are about others
We are certainly laboring for people

We don't immediately know
In the space that we make

Our life is a space
Others answer after us

```
t  r  u  s  t            t  r  u  s  t            t  r  u  s  t            t  r  u  s  t
r           r            r           r            r           r            r           r
u           u            u           u            u           u            u           u
s           s            s           s            s           s            s           s
t  r  u  s  t  r  u  s  t  r  u  s  t  r  u  s  t  r  u  s  t  r  u  s  t  r  u  s  t
            r           r           r           r           r           r
            u           u           u           u           u           u
            s           s           s           s           s           s
t  r  u  s  t  r  u  s  t  r  u  s  t  r  u  s  t  r  u  s  t  r  u  s  t  r  u  s  t
r           r           r           r           r           r           r           r
u           u           u           u           u           u           u           u
s           s           s           s           s           s           s           s
t  r  u  s  t  r  u  s  t  r  u  s  t  r  u  s  t  r  u  s  t  r  u  s  t  r  u  s  t
            r           r           r           r           r           r
            u           u           u           u           u           u
            s           s           s           s           s           s
t  r  u  s  t  r  u  s  t  r  u  s  t  r  u  s  t  r  u  s  t  r  u  s  t  r  u  s  t
r           r           r           r           r           r           r           r
u           u           u           u           u           u           u           u
s           s           s           s           s           s           s           s
t  r  u  s  t  r  u  s  t  r  u  s  t  r  u  s  t  r  u  s  t  r  u  s  t  r  u  s  t
            r           r           r           r           r           r
            u           u           u           u           u           u
            s           s           s           s           s           s
t  r  u  s  t  r  u  s  t  r  u  s  t  r  u  s  t  r  u  s  t  r  u  s  t  r  u  s  t
r           r           r           r           r           r           r           r
u           u           u           u           u           u           u           u
s           s           s           s           s           s           s           s
t  r  u  s  t  r  u  r  t  r  u  s  t  r  u  r  t  r  u  s  t  r  u  r  t  r  u  s  t
            r           r           r           r           r
            u           u           u           u           u
            s           s           s           s           s
t  r  u  s  t  r  u  r  t  r  u  s  t  r  u  r  t  r  u  s  t  r  u  r  t  r  u  s  t
r           r           r           r           r           r           r           r
u           u           u           u           u           u           u           u
s           s           s           s           s           s           s           s
t  r  u  s  t  r  u  r  t  r  u  s  t  r  u  r  t  r  u  s  t  r  u  r  t  r  u  s  t
            r           r           r           r           r
            u           u           u           u           u
            s           s           s           s           s
t  r  u  s  t  r  u  r  t  r  u  s  t  r  u  r  t  r  u  s  t  r  u  r  t  r  u  s  t
r           r           r           r           r           r           r           r
u           u           u           u           u           u           u           u
s           s           s           s           s           s           s           s
t  r  u  s  t            t  r  u  s  t            t  r  u  s  t            t  r  u  s  t
```

```
t  r  u  s  t           t  r  u  s  t           t  r  u  s  t           t  r  u  s  t
r           r           r           r           r           r           r           r
u           u           u           u           u           u           u           u
s           s           s           s           s           s           s           s
t  r  u  s  t  r  u  s  t  r  u  s  t  r  u  s  t  r  u  s  t  r  u  s  t  r  u  s  t
            r           r           r           r           r           r
            u           u           u           u           u           u
            s           s           s           s           s           s
t  r  u  s  t  r  u  s  t  r  u  s  t  r  u  s  t  r  u  s  t  r  u  s  t  r  u  s  t
r           r           r           r           r           r           r           r
u           u           u           u           u           u           u           u
s           s           s           s           s           s           s           s
t  r  u  s  t  r  u  s  t  r  u  s  t  r  u  s  t  r  u  s  t  r  u  s  t  r  u  s  t
            r           r           r           r           r           r
            u           u           u           u           u           u
            s           s           s           s           s           s
t  r  u  s  t  r  u  s  t  r  u  s  t  r  u  s  t  r  u  s  t  r  u  s  t  r  u  s  t
r           r           r           r           r           r           r           r
u           u           u           u           u           u           u           u
s           s           s           s           s           s           s           s
t  r  u  s  t  r  u  s  t  r  u  s  t  r  u  s  t  r  u  s  t  r  u  s  t  r  u  s  t
            r           r           r           r           r           r
            u           u           u           u           u           u
            s           s           s           s           s           s
t  r  u  s  t  r  u  s  t  r  u  s  t  r  u  s  t  r  u  s  t  r  u  s  t  r  u  s  t
r           r           r           r           r           r           r           r
u           u           u           u           u           u           u           u
s           s           s           s           s           s           s           s
t  r  u  s  t  r  u  r  t  r  u  s  t  r  u  r  t  r  u  s  t  r  u  r  t  r  u  s  t
            r           r           r           r           r
            u           u           u           u           u
            s           s           s           s           s
t  r  u  s  t  r  u  r  t  r  u  s  t  r  u  r  t  r  u  s  t  r  u  r  t  r  u  s  t
r           r           r           r           r           r           r           r
u           u           u           u           u           u           u           u
s           s           s           s           s           s           s           s
t  r  u  s  t  r  u  r  t  r  u  s  t  r  u  r  t  r  u  s  t  r  u  r  t  r  u  s  t
            r           r           r           r           r
            u           u           u           u           u
            s           s           s           s           s
t  r  u  s  t  r  u  r  t  r  u  s  t  r  u  r  t  r  u  s  t  r  u  r  t  r  u  s  t
r           r           r           r           r           r           r           r
u           u           u           u           u           u           u           u
s           s           s           s           s           s           s           s
t  r  u  s  t           t  r  u  s  t           t  r  u  s  t           t  r  u  s  t
```

Acknowledgements

to Nick Courtright, Kyle McCord, & Cammie Finch
for welcoming me to Atmosphere

to Frank Montesonti, Marci Rae Johnson, and Michael
Rerick for shaping the pieces of this manuscript &

to the editors for first choosing these pieces

Wingless Dreamer International Poetry Contest Finalist,
Winter 2020, Aegis of Waves

Monday Journal, Winter 2020
Storm & Stress, Valence, Trust

Tempered Runes, Fall 2020
Mis Quinces II & I

Fieldstone Review, Fall 2020
Digital Narcosis

Peauxdunque Review, October 2020
They Think They Are White

Poetry Pea, July 2020
Sutter Buttes Haibun

Poet's Choice, July 2020
House on Fire

Finding the Birds, June 2020
My Name Is Adam

Father and I, (Ruchi Acharya, Ed.), June 2020
Fathers With Their Sons

Cathix Northwest Press, October 2018
El Viaje —The Journey—Transition

Sixfold Poetry, Winter 2018
Lost Rites, Male Initiation Rites, Female Initiation Rites,
Putressence, #marchforourlives

Heart and Humanity, September 2018
Iftar Ghazal and Quality of Life

About Atmosphere Press

Atmosphere Press is an independent, full-service publisher for excellent books in all genres and for all audiences. Learn more about what we do at atmospherepress.com.

We encourage you to check out some of Atmosphere's latest releases, which are available at Amazon.com and via order from your local bookstore:

The Distance from Odessa, poetry by Carol Seitchik
How It Shone, poetry by Katherine Barham
Wind Bells, poetry in English and Tagalog by Jessica Perez Dimalibot
Meraki, poetry by Tobi-Hope Jieun Park
Impression, poetry by Charnjit Gill
Aching to be Human, poetry by Stormy Abel
Love is Blood, Love is Fabric, poetry by Mary De La Fuente
How to Hypnotize a Lobster, poetry by Kristin Rose Jutras
The Mercer Stands Burning, night poems by John Pietaro
Calls for Help, poetry by Greg T. Miraglia
Lost in the Greenwood, poetry by Ellen Roberts Young
Blessed Arrangement, poetry by Larry Levy
Lovely Dregs, poetry by Richard Sipe
Out of the Dark, poetry by William Guest
Shadow Truths, poetry by V. Rendina
A Synonym for Home, poetry by Kimberly Jarchow
The Cry of Being Born, poetry by Carol Mariano
Big Man Small Europe, poetry by Tristan Niskanen
Lucid_Malware.zip, poetry by Dylan Sonderman
The Unordering of Days, poetry by Jessica Palmer
It's Not About You, poetry by Daniel Casey
A Dream of Wide Water, poetry by Sharon Whitehill
Radical Dances of the Ferocious Kind, poetry by Tina Tru

Elder Gideon holds an MFA in poetry, builds an iconography cooperative Sophia Guild, guides underserved high school English students, and grows the Sophian Tradition as a disciple of Tau Malachi, with whom he co-authored "Gnosis of Guadalupe" (EPS Press, 2017). Elder Gideon thrives in collaboration, producing, directing, and performing his chapbook "Owl Songs" set to original music by Sean Wall. This is available on all music streaming services. Collaborating with Sean Wall, and Canadian filmmaker Bevan Klassen, Elder Gideon produced and narrated an experimental documentary "Dark Before Dawn," which debuted with Woven Tale Press summer 2020. *Aegis of Waves* is his first book.

Visit *eldergideon.com*, or say hello at *eldergideon@gmail.com*.